P9-CAJ-725

Island Lake
Catskiing
2013
25th Anniversary

Text:
Mike McPhee, Mark Gallup, Leslie Anthony and Lee-Anne Walker

Photos:
Mark Gallup, Henry Georgi, Jeff Patterson, Eric Berger,
Trevor Graves, Jeff Curtis, Matt Kuhn, Aaron Whitfield, Dano Pendygrasse, Dave Silver,
Tony Harrington and Mike McPhee

Designed and fretted over by:
Mike McPhee

Edited by:
Carolyn Nikodym, Carissa Hart and Marie-Kristine Landry

Publisher
Oolichan Books

Craig Kelly bringing his surfer-style to a powder wave near Tua Time, a large feature in upper Geisha Bowl. *Photo: Mark Gallup*

Looking at the Upper Nonstop snowcat drop-off point from Cyclops.
Photo: Henry Georgi

Contents:

Forward ***by Leslie Anthony***

Introduction ***by Mike McPhee***

Timeline 12

Craig Kelly's first time ***by Mark Gallup*** 16

Photo Gallery 20

Cats and Characters 52

Scot Schmidt 64

Magazine Covers 68

Silver Screen 75

The Fifth Element 80

Natural History of the Cedar Valley 88

Summer Story 92

Endtro 94

Cover Photo Story and inset (Bryan Iguchi with painting)
Bryan Iguchi and Terje Haakonson arrived at the Lodge in March of 1996 for a Burton photo shoot. Having just seen the Baby Bear and moon photo published in *Transworld Snowboarding Magazine*, Bryan wanted a large print of it for his house in Jackson Hole. I said, "how about we do a trade?" Bryan was a budding artist at the time and had all his painting materials with him. By the end of the week, Bryan completed his rendition of the photograph. I'm pretty sure I got the better deal! — *Mark Gallup*

Forward by Leslie Anthony

Island Lake Lodge: *a measure of legend*

During any of snowsport's many epochs, a world of possibility and direction has made itself visible through some newly minted lens. In the early '90s, that lens was Island Lake Lodge.

It wasn't that catskiing was anything new—though Island Lake Mountain Tours, as it was then known, was one of the earliest entries (and icons) in what became a very populous field. And it wasn't that other places like, say, Alaska couldn't spare room for us all—only that the great white beyond and its promise of endless first descents and bottomless powder was too far and too expensive for all but the pros and bros of the ski and snowboard film fraternity.

It was, however, this same video industry—driven by the success of snowboarding, the *Steep & Deep* ethos portrayed in Greg Stump's landmark *Blizzard of Aahhhs*, and a continental clamour for ski areas to open their boundaries—that created a public desire for alpine and cultural discovery, and an interest in off-piste that followed the visual promise of the Alps and Alaska—uncountable peaks, precipitous faces, untracked snow, few humans. More mountainous yet far more accessible, the sleepy Canadian province of British Columbia became a stand-in for all of this. With magazine-and-movie fascination focused around the so-called Powder Triangle of Fernie, Whitewater and Red Mountain, an unpretentious troika of smallish resorts in southeast B.C., interest naturally found its way to the unique topography and microclimate of the Cedar Valley and a low-key cat-ski operation called Island Lake.

The visionaries behind this labour of love created something that changed the mechanized backcountry industry. And the difference would be Island Lake's relationship to the industry. With snowboarding exploding and skiing forced to compete on every front, a sudden glut of movies and magazines cried out for new stories in spectacular places. Embracing this burgeoning demand, Island Lake made an investment in the future that no other operation had thought to do: they simply invited everyone.

As one of those pilgrims, along with Henry Georgi my frequent photo collaborator of the time (now a Fernie resident), I'll take some credit (or blame, depending on your perspective) for blowing up Island Lake. It has been claimed that bookings increased by some 750 per cent following my feature "Still Life with Lizard" in the November 1993 issue of *Powder*. Myth or not, it certainly says less about my powers of persuasion than a marketplace suddenly alerted to its perfect object of affection: the very definition of steep and deep.

The Lizard Range in all its glory, as seen from Mt. Fernie.
Photo: Henry Georgi

That was because skiing at Island Lake, just over the imposing alabaster ramparts of the Lizard Range from Fernie, made the precipitous slopes of even that powder paradise seem pedestrian. On my first trip in, grinding along in a cat during heavy snowfall, ancient cedars of coastal proportions rose beside us like living totems, testament to a unique microclimate where East-West and North-South valleys met to funnel precipitation in from all directions. The snowfall and forest were magic, but when we rounded the final corner to behold the hand-hewn, peeled-log splendour of the lodge, I was sold.

By promoting a relationship with every major snow media, Island Lake went from a five-year struggle to a three-year waiting list. The two biggest stars of the time, skier Scot Schmidt and snowboarder Craig Kelly, both invested. Whether chicken or egg, Island Lake became one of the first places skiers and boarders filmed together, a thread that Stump picked up in his film *Siberia*. The relevance of this synergy can't be understated. Turnstile meetings of skiers like Schmidt, Trevor Petersen, Eric Pehota, Seth Morrison and the globetrotting Egan brothers, with snowboard heavyweights like Kelly, Jason Ford and Terje Haakonsen, and photo icons like Henry Georgi, Mark Gallup and Scott Markewitz transformed Island Lake into the kind of industry nexus usually reserved for large resorts. Movies like the Egan brothers' *Extreme Dream,* Stump's *P-Tex, Lies and Duct Tape*, and MSP's *Fetish* contained some of the deepest, most transformative footage produced at the time. Honouring this legacy, Island Lake remains a venue for cutting-edge filmmaking: a good deal of the mind-blowing footage from the Sherpa's ground-breaking, multi-award-winning 2012 joint, *All.I.Can,* was shot here.

Back in the day, our welcome was a run off Baldy Peak down Suntanner, a plunging ridge of thinned trees; our second Swiss Run, a gem that alternated between dwarf evergreens and open expanses peppered by snags and snow-ghosts with room to open up, gather speed and choose which trees to sweep around. There was Enchanted Forest on Lower Baldy, and on the other side of the Valley, below the most outrageous alpine bowls known to cat-skiers at the time, shots through old-growth giants in spaces wide enough to drive a truck through. Roller-coastering over enormous downed trunks, pillow stumps and hero cliffs in the deepest snow we'd ever skied was serious skiing that allowed for almost child-like fun, which, in the end, is probably behind most of Island Lake's lasting mystique.

No matter the epoch, no matter the lens, riding snow is all about fun. And the newfound fun at Island Lake in the early '90s will always be legendary.

Intro by Mike McPhee

The limestone spires of the Three Bears rise above Island Lake like sentinels guarding a secret place. The meandering approach through snow-caked old growth forest and alongside a bubbling brook adds to electric anticipation, which always impresses first-timers and veterans alike. Grizzly bears, cougars, elk and moose prowl the pristine valley as they have for millennia. Though only a few miles from Fernie, B.C., the Cedar Valley, in which Island Lake sits, is its own magical world. The local micro-climate produces an unusual amount of snow for even this part of the Rocky Mountains, adding to the reputation of one of the most legendary backcountry lodges in North America…Island Lake Lodge Catskiing.

I first learned to ski and snowboard on the "hills" of Manitoba. The big mountains out West and the characters that rode them held an almost mythical place in my psyche. It was the early '90s and snowboarding was injecting newfound energy and passion into the snowsports industry. A couple of friends owned a skateboard/snowboard shop and had all the latest magazines and videos. We spent youthful hours studying the new styles, tricks and trends. There was a destination that seemed to garner the most photos in every magazine and every video seemed to include obligatory segment in order for it to be legit. For us eager and willing youngsters, Island Lake seemed to be the epicentre of the ski and snowboard industry. When referring to big mountain riding, my friends and I started referring to it as "Island Lake Style." It represented all the possibilities and aspirations that the big mountains out West had to offer—and, of course, glorious deep powder accessed by snowcat.

Eventually the call of the big mountains enthralled me and the time came to take the plunge. I can honestly say that Island Lake Lodge and Mark Gallup's photos of the place inspired me to move west and follow my passions in the mountains of British Columbia. One exploratory season became 17, and I find myself deeply rooted in the once mythical place that drew me west in the first place.

Coming full circle—researching this book, exploring Island Lake and Mark Gallup's archives and slide library has been like time travelling to the exuberant

Callum Pettit and Eric Hjorliefson preparing for powder.
Photo: Mike McPhee

The beauty of snow-caked trees on a stormy day. *Photo: Mike McPhee*

days of adolescence, when everything was charged with a special anticipation and optimism. It was hard not to feel giddy and reminiscent as I thumbed through the original slides of the classic shots that had inspired a whole generation of skiers and snowboarders. The wonder and awe of seeing big air, big lines and über-deep champagne powder in those early days came rushing back.

In recent years our collective psyches may have become a bit jaded with overhyped pros and their double-cork everythings, but this exercise reminded me (and I hope you) of the soul and inspiration that brought us here and motivated us in the first place. I am also reminded of the volume of interesting characters that have evolved and succeeded in the industry over the years, unique individuals that broke trail for the rest of us and were energized by being on the tip of something new. These characters literally were and are responsible for how and what we ride today. The archives are an interesting testament to the power that a unique place can have over people and the media. Not only did I come across thousands of editorial photos from Island Lake Lodge, but truckloads of advertising shots as well. Over time, it slowly dawned on me that the history of Island Lake is closely connected to the history of snowboarding itself and has played a key role in the turning point of a new, vibrant ski industry in general. Craig Kelly's transformation from a competition-focused rider to big mountain freeriding legend was virtually blueprinted here. He famously turned his back on the accepted role of a pro and went deeper into the mountains for solace. Scot Schmidt brought his new freeskiing style and confidence to the Lodge at an early stage and documented it here with equally head-turning results. Perhaps most profoundly, Scot and Craig decided to bring snowboard and ski culture together on film, right here in the Lizard Range at Island Lake, and ultimately, both became shareholders, directors and regulars around the fireplace. I am always interested to hear from industry icons that it does not matter what you ride, that it really is all about the experience of being in and enjoying the mountains.

Many of the big mountain riders who were changing the course of the industry were making their mark here and having photos published with the location credit, "Island Lake Lodge, Fernie, B.C." The Egan Brothers filmed their first full-length movie *The Extreme Dream*; Greg Stump filmed his groundbreaking movie *P-Tex, Lies and Duct Tape*. MSP and the Warren Miller franchise both followed suit and filmed epic segments shortly after. Things have recently come around full circle with Sherpas Cinema filming a portion of their seminal and award-winning film *All.I.CAN* at Island Lake and sister company Mica Heliskiing.

Over the years Island Lake Lodge has inspired a generation (or two) of snow-sliding enthusiasts. It has given many a "best day ever" to guests and still stands tall in the upper reaches of the Cedar Valley. 2013 will mark 25 years of catskiing at Island Lake, and it seems fitting to celebrate and document this milestone with a book.

An aerial perspective of the backside of Lizard Range. *Photo: Matt Kuhn*

Timeline

Pre European Settlers - Ktunaxa First Nation People passed through the area on a regular basis, but did not settle.

Circa 1874 - Prospector and trapper Michael Phillips names Lizard Creek for the "little green lizards" he finds at the head waters. He is said to be the first European to traverse Crowsnest Pass.

1897 - William Fernie and others start extracting coal in the Elk Valley.

1902 - The Cedar Valley Improvement Co. starts logging operations in the lower Cedar Valley, which is now part of the Island Lake property.

1904 - Fernie's Downtown burns to the ground, prompting the incorporation of the City of Fernie.

1905 - The property of the Cedar Valley Improvement Co. is sold to F.H. Hale. Changes name to The North American Land & Lumber Co.

Early 1900s
Locals build a small day-use cabin at Island Lake.

1908 - The entire city of Fernie burns down.

1914 - The Fernie Alpine Club makes the suggestion that Island Lake be stocked with fish and a preserve put on the lake.

1917 - The Fernie Alpine Club leases Island Lake and the surrounding territory from the lumber company for the enjoyment of its members.

1920 - A short rail-line is built up the lower Cedar Valley to haul logs.

Winter 1967/68 - Geisha House is built on the site of the current lodges from rough-hewn logs by some local forestry workers. It's damaged by fire and is never finished.

1904 - 1924 - Photographer Joseph F. Spalding photographs Fernie and the area, including a few visits to Island Lake. He is one of the first people to start talking about tourism in the area.

Late 1940s - Skiing becomes a popular pastime and locals make good use of the trails up to Island Lake.

1955 - The Snow Valley Ski Association is formed by local enthusiasts.

1920s - 1930s - Locals continue to hunt, fish and enjoy the lands around Island Lake. Logging continues on the lower property. Forest fires continue to change the landscape but leave most of the upper Cedar Valley untouched.

1960-61 - Fernie bids on winter Olympics.

Late 1940s - Below is the first known "action ski shot" from Island Lake. Notice Mount Baldy in the background.

1962 - A group of local skiers builds Snow Valley Ski Hill, later named Fernie Alpine Resort, just a few kms from Island Lake.

Timeline

1975 - Alan Drury starts the first commercial catski operation at Selkirk Wilderness Skiing.

1985 - Dan McDonald and Rod Pendlebury start with the idea of ski touring and cross-country skiing around Island Lake and the Lizard Range.

1986/7 - Mark Gallup comes up ski touring for the first time and sees the potential.

1987/88 - The Bear Lodge is constructed. The original lodge is where guests, ate, slept and enjoyed aprés-ski. The company name at this time is Island Lake Mountain Tours

1988 - The first snowcat is delivered and catskiing starts at Island Lake Lodge.

1992 - Mark Gallup brings Craig Kelly to Island Lake for the first time. Craig is impressed and tells Scot Schmidt about it soon after.

1994 - Greg Stump films *P-Tex, Lies and Duct Tape* with Craig Kelly and Scot Schmidt. Mark Gallup takes a number of signature photos.

1995 - Shell Canada, who was leasing the land to Island Lake, puts the entire 7,000 acres up for sale. Dan McDonald and current partners, Dale Bowman and Bob Langfield have 30 days to come up with the money. They end up putting together a group of investors at the 11th hour.

1995 - Red Eagle Lodge is built. This allows expanded accommodation.

1996 - 2000
Scot Schmidt and others hold The Gathering, a summer music Festival.

2001 - 2003
Jake Blattner holds the "Summer Jam Sessions" — exclusive snow camps in the upper bowls.

2002 - The Cedar Lodge is built.

2005 - The Tamarack Lodge is built, adding more rooms, full spa and a larger dining room.

2010/11 - Sherpas Cinema film a large portion of their award winning movie *ALL.I.CAN* at Island Lake and Mica Heliskiing. They also produce a TV show — *The Balance of Powder* for the 2 operations.

1996 - MSP films *Fetish*. Seth Morrison is filmed coming down Big White in one of the deepest segments most people had seen at the time.

1999 - Island Lake starts to open regularly for summer.

2002 - Warren Miller films a segment of *Ride* at Island Lake with Craig Kelly and Jonovan Moore.

2002 - Island Lake purchases another operation and brands it *Powder Cowboy Catskiing.*

2002 - Teton Gravity Research films a segment of their movie *The Prophecy* with Scot Schmidt, Micah Black and Travis Rice.

2005 - The Shareholder group sells to a new majority owner Patrick Callahan. This new owner brings Mica Heliskiing into the fold.

2008 - Island Lake, several past chefs and author Keith Liggett publish a gourmet cookbook.

Craig Kelly's First Time by Mark Gallup

The first time I met Craig Kelly was at the Calgary airport. A few weeks earlier, Burton called and said that Craig wanted to make a transition from his race career to freeride. I don't think we even used the term "freeride" back then, but this was the direction Craig wanted to go. The powers at Burton kept a close eye on all media, including the ski magazines, and they pegged me as the backcountry guy that could get the powder shots they needed of Craig.

"Do you have a powder location you can take Craig to?" inquired the voice on the other end.

"Yes, I have the perfect place. It's a powder mecca!" I said.

A tired, worn out Craig got into my Volvo station wagon that night at the airport. He said very little. I mentioned that the drive would take about three hours. This was followed by awkward silence. I put the Volvo through the gears and stuck in a cassette tape. This now left only space for conversation.

"Are you hungry?" I asked.

Craig with musician Lester Quitzau on one of his first trips to Island Lake. *Photo: Mark Gallup*

"Butter tarts," he said. He finally cracked a smile. "You Canadians have those butter tarts at your gas stations."

After a stop at 7-11 for gas and a feeding of butter tarts, we drove into the night and our 20-year friendship began.

There were two sides to Craig. Actually there were several sides, including his evil, practical joke side. But the two sides I'm referring to are his public side and his private side. Probably pretty common for somebody in his position, he chose his words well for the public, said the right things and was a professional through and through. This was his default side, that is, until he got to know someone. Once the trust was there, there were seemingly no boundaries.

But let's back up a little bit, back to that night I first picked him up at the airport. At the time, there was only one way to make a living in snowboarding, and that was to compete. Burton had their doubts about him making this change into uncharted territories. But by this time, Craig could do no wrong in their eyes. And they supported him. I didn't know it at the time, and maybe even Craig didn't know it at the time, but he had a plan. We were about to find out it was going to be groundbreaking.

We awoke to the Lizard Range doing what it does best, blowing people's minds! It was a classic Island Lake sunrise. I still think this was the turning point for Craig in many ways. Up to this point Craig had been to Canada, mostly the West Coast as a competitor, but this trip might have been the first time he realized there was a lot more. Island Lake showed us her A game and by the end of our tour, Craig was hooked and wanting more.

Busy schedule: Craig couldn't return until two years later. When he finally made it back, he brought filmer Greg Stump and legendary skier Scot Schmidt. Craig and Scot met during a film trip to Siberia and Craig told Scot about this amazing place in Fernie, B.C. Like the first time, Island Lake met all expectations. The crew filmed what is considered a pinnacle sequence of the time. It sounds strange now, but shooting a sequence of a skier and snowboarder riding together was cutting edge! Greg Stump's film *P-tex, Lies and Duct Tape*

Craig Kelly attacking the fall line like only Craig could. Filming Greg Stump's *P-Tex, lies and Duct Tape* and his second time at Island Lake, it was the beginning of an amazing relationship.
Photo: Mark Gallup

brought Island lake Lodge to the cinema for the first time.

After this second success, Island Lake became an obsession for Craig. He found any excuse to get back to Island Lake. His plan had worked. His career as a champion competitor was now overshadowed by Craig Kelly: backcountry guru and Island Lake was his template.

In 1995, the owners at the time told us that the land was for sale and they wanted new shareholders. In a few short years, Island Lake was on the international map, a household name plastered all over the ski and snowboard magazines; by now many snow-famous people had experienced it. That is where owners went looking for investors. They called up known names like Scot Schmidt, Jason Ford, Jake Blattner and, of course, Craig Kelly. Without hesitation we all became shareholders. Once again Island Lake was cutting fresh tracks, this time with "rock star" athletes as owners: a brilliant marketing move that would be emulated by followers.

Here, the Craig Kelly and Island Lake story hits its peak. On January 20th, 2003, Craig's life would reach a tragic end. Since Craig always had a plan, he saw his next natural step: to use his backcountry experience to become the first ACMG-certified snowboard guide. It was on this new journey that he fully and finally experienced everything the mountains offered.

Craig broke ground with the freeride revolution. He broke ground taking the business of being a professional snowboarder to the next level. And he broke ground legitimizing snowboarders in the world of guiding. His legend becomes stronger as every year passes.

I often think back to those first awkward hours in the Volvo driving to Fernie. In the next two decades that followed we became close friends. I got to know his private side, his practical-joker side, his incredible abilities as an athlete and as a forward-thinker. There is no doubt that Craig was a true artist in his craft. But every artist needs a canvas and for Craig, that canvas was Island Lake Lodge.

For over a decade, Island Lake was a white canvas for Craig, honing his skills on the snow and in the business of snow. *Photo: Mark Gallup*

At home on the steeps. *Photo: Mark Gallup*

The unquestionable king of style. *Photo: Mark Gallup*

A quick portrait before hopping in a helicopter to explore the Lizard Range and the surrounding area.
Photo: Mark Gallup

Photo Gallery

An early morning crew hikes up the ridge on Tua Time to catch the golden light.
Photo: Mark Gallup

The day after a big storm, guide Steve Kujit leads a group down the face from Geisha High Tree.
Photo: Mark Gallup

All snow is deep on those skis! Scot Schmidt blasting through the powder during the filming of *P-tex, Lies and Duct Tape* circa 1994. Scot brought a lot to the table in his shareholder days, such as The Gathering music festival. He still visits every winter. *Photo: Mark Gallup*

Eric Pehota was Trevor Petersen's ski mountaineer partner and shared many first descents with him all over the world. An absolute powerhouse of his time, he stepped up to any challenge the mountains put in front of him. The term "extreme skier" was the best description of both Eric and Trevor before the term became over-used!
Photo: Mark Gallup

It didn't take long for Island Lake Lodge to become a household name in the world of powder junkies, and many ski and snowboard stars wanted a piece of the action, like Eric DesLauriers and Dan Egan. *Photo Mark Gallup*

Legends of the snowboard world, Jamie Lynn and Axel Pauporté walked up this chute just above Geisha High Tree for a little morning warm up.
Photo: Mark Gallup

Considered one of the best ski mountaineers of his time, Trevor Petersen made a living making first descents. He was also pretty good at first tracks! *Photo: Mark Gallup*

Jake Blattner getting it done on what was nicknamed "The Movie Slope" because it was where all the film crews went. It's the perfect combination of amazing morning light, steep wind lip, and epic background. Seen in hundreds of magazines and films. *Photo: Mark Gallup*

Snowboarding made its debut at the 1998 Olympics in Nagano, afterwards, the U.S. snowboard team came up to Island Lake for a photo shoot and a little break from the hype. Carabeth Burnside didn't win gold, but she was going for it on this roller in Geisha Bowl.
Photo: Mark Gallup

One of the best things about catskiing is shredding with your buddies.
Photo: Mark Gallup

Both photos on this page — Seth Morrison's first visit was in 1996 with MSP and an all-star cast of skiers. Though Alaska was all over the ski movies at the time, Seth's powder segment from Island Lake became legendary. *Photo: Mark Gallup*

Canadian Snowboard pioneer Ken Achenbach arrived on the scene in the early years of Island Lake.
Photo: Mark Gallup

Probably the only time this was ever done, Mike Orr looked at this famous landmark on Spineback Ridge a little differently then others. *Photo: Mark Gallup*

Every year, *Transworld Snowboarding* magazine dedicates an entire issue to interviews. In 1997, the seven top riders of the year, along with the editors, writers and senior photographers of *TWS,* converged on Island Lake's playground. Riders included Jeremy Jones, Shin Campos and Ian Spiro shown here straight-lining Cyclops. Island Lake's longest-standing guide Corrie Wright stands watch from the peak. *Photo: Mark Gallup*

Canadian ski pioneer Trevor Petersen came across this cliff while exploring the Mt. Fernie side. Only accessed by helicopter or ski touring at the time, the operation has now expanded into this area with some great tree skiing.
Photo: Mark Gallup

Kye Petersen with a creative tree tap while filming with Sherpas Cinema, opposite his legendary father Trevor Petersen.
Photo: Mike McPhee

Craig Kelly on the iconic Spineback Ridge chute.
Photo: Mark Gallup

Jonaven Moore pays tribute on Craig's Chute.
Photo: Jeff Patterson

A few of Island Lake's Guides hard at work! *Photo: Mark Gallup*

You could spot Craig's style a mile away! And I think the camera WAS about a mile away for this one. Craig was truly the master of the natural terrain.
Photo: Mark Gallup

Ross Peterson welcomes the sunrise with a method
on the slopes above Tua Time. *Photo: Mark Gallup*

Dave Treadway finds some nice light in the "Movie Slope" area. *Photo: Eric Berger*

Eero Niemela shows some Euro style with a big spin into the Gun Barrel.
Photo: Mike McPhee

Eric Hjorliefson.
Photo: Mike McPhee

Murray Hodgson spins over a cat-road gap on a stormy day during a shoot for *Snowboard Canada* magazine. *Photo: Jeff Patterson*

Eric Hjorleifson displays some proper Schmidt-esque style while shooting with Sherpas Cinema. *Photo: Mike McPhee*

Sean Pettit has quickly gained a reputation of bringing new school tricks and style to the backcountry. *Photo: Mike McPhee*

Cats, Characters & Lodges

You can sometimes see character in the geography of a place and feel it in the air. Character shines with subtle differences allowing something or someone to stand out from the rest. In this story, the characters include the log lodges, the rugged snowcats, the assortment of interesting people and, of course, the landscape. From the early trappers and prospectors to gun-slinging, rum-drinking loggers all the way to the present age of pro skiers and powder hounds, Island Lake Lodge and the Cedar Valley have witnessed a full cast of interesting characters.

Michael Phillips was one of the first, if not the first, trapper/prospector to explore the Fernie area. He spent the summer of 1874 in the Elk Valley and explored many of the tributary creeks, including Lizard Creek. He named it after the little green lizards (salamanders) he found at the headwaters, which is right beside Island Lake. He named a few other creeks of the area, including Morrissey and Coal Creek, and was also the first European to discover Crowsnest Pass. Phillips discovered coal around Fernie and then gold in the Bull River. He documented accessing the Bull River through Iron Creek and Iron Pass, which are within the Island Lake property. Sam Steele, the famous RCMP officer and western legend, camped at the junction of Lizard Creek and the Elk River in the summer of 1888. There is a cedar tree on the Island Lake property with "Steele" carved into it and an RCMP chevron. While it appears to be genuine, it is not yet confirmed to be his handiwork—though it very well could be.

The Little Lodge in the woods. *Photo: Mark Gallup*

The lodges themselves are lead characters in this story. The log buildings are built to withstand the rugged environment and provide a cozy refuge for guests. There was a small day-use cabin on the lake in the early 1900s; however, the origins of the modern lodges trace their beginning to the winter of 1967-68, when a log building referred to as "Geisha House" was built on the site of the current lodges. Crows Nest Industries logging crews went on strike in the summer of 1967, so Heiko Socher (who built the modern Fernie ski hill) was asked to construct a lodge with his foremen of the logging crews. They cut the trees right there at the site, had a portable saw pulled to Island Lake and cut 10' by 10' timbers to build Geisha House. Unfortunately it was damaged by fire before it could be finished or occupied. The story goes that some of the wives in town started calling it the Geisha House, as their husbands would disappear up to Island Lake to work on the mysterious building for many a long day.

In 1987-88, Bear Lodge was built. Constructed from Western larch logs harvested near Hosmer, the building

Fernie Free Press - October 3, 1903

Thos. Dunn was up for trial on Wednesday in connection with the scrap he got into at the Cedar Valley Improvement Company's stable last week. Only one charge was laid, that of pointing a firearm with intent to do injury. He was unable to put up any defence, but as his employers spoke favourably of him and as it was shown that he was under the influence of liquor at the time, the magistrate viewed the offence with leniency and allowed him to go with a fine of $50 which he paid.

was cut and formed in Fernie, then taken apart and transported up the road to its current location. The inside of the lodge has been transformed a few times to suit different needs. Originally it was the only lodge, where all of the guests and staff ate, slept and dried their gear. A large wood stove on the main floor heated the entire structure. The upper level consisted of spartan rooms with bunk beds and a couple of communal washrooms and showers. In the early '90s a friend of Scot Schmidt's built the grand river-rock fireplace you see today. The striking blue and red rock is from the Wigwam River, south of Fernie. Today the Bear Lodge is a bar/après-ski lounge in the evening, with the guide's office and gear rooms located in the basement.

In 1995, Red Eagle Lodge was constructed across the meadow from the Bear, adding more accommodation. The Lodge is named after Kootenai Chief Red Eagle, who lifted a nineteenth century curse on Fernie in 1964. The curse was blamed for the town flooding and burning down a couple of times. Originally equipped with its own kitchen, the Red Eagle has also been transformed a few times over the years. More accommodation was added with beautiful Cedar Lodge in 2000. The Cedar has eight rooms and a conference/stretching room downstairs. Five years later the Tamarack Lodge was built. With the main dining room, kitchen and full spa downstairs, it is now the central hub of Island Lake. All of the lodges are built in the classic Canadian Rockies log building style: sizable larch and Douglas fir logs are accented with river rock. In an effort to lessen Island Lake Lodge's footprint, the entire operation runs on micro hydroelectricity, which generates 70 kilowatts from two hydro stations.

Over the 25 years of catskiing, there has been an interesting progression of snowcats as well. The first cat was an old Thiokol, which was used only as transport to the Lodge. Then a PistenBully 200 was purchased from Heiko. This was the first cat that drove up into the terrain and was used for catskiing. Later, a PistenBully 240 was purchased from Charlie Locke, owner of Lake Louise Mountain Resort. Today, Island Lake has three PistenBully 250s, each with a custom carrier on the back for transporting skiers and snowboarders. The comfortable

Fernie Free Press - August 19, 1910
- GOT THE HOOK!

Billy Perdue had a novel experience with a bear on Tuesday afternoon. He was fishing along Lizard Creek, working upstream, and was whipping a pool below a little waterfall that made a brawling noise in the woods... Billy had no luck in the lower pool and cast his flies over the logs to have a stealthy try at the hole higher up. Suddenly he felt a tug on his line and the next moment the last section of his rod and the most of his line went with a snap and a small black bear shot into the bushes. Simultaneously a twelve inch trout was jerked from the water and leaped after the bear. Billy figures that the bear was lying on a small gravel bar above the logs probably asleep. When the trout took the last fly on the cast it jerked one of the other flies across the nose of the ursine sleeper. Billy thinks that if he had known the strike he was going to get he may have played him to a better advantage.

Early locals enjoying the lake.
- Photo: Courtesy of the Fernie Museum

carriers have sound systems with iPod players and lots of room for food, drinks and gear. There is also a road-building cat and transportation cat in the fleet, which are both PistenBullies as well.

Nobody on record can recall when the Three Bears were named, but they were probably named by one of the early European explorers. They are certainly signature peaks that stand out from the rest of the Lizard Range. Their limestone spire bodies step forward from the main ridgeline, and they appear to rise above all others with purpose. The peaks get side-lit with deep, warm alpenglow at sunrise and sunset, creating an image that is guaranteed to stay burned in your memory for many years. Like the many personalities of this story, they tower larger than life over the valley.

While it's hard to ignore the many big-name skiers and snowboarders who have enjoyed riding Island Lake's terrain, the interesting mix of guests over the years cannot be overlooked. Many have become addicted to the experience and have come back year after year, with a few going on 20 years of consecutive catskiing vacations. The passion for Island Lake is clearly illustrated by the fact that some guests went on to become shareholders and have made contributions of various kinds to the operation. Not only did people ski the pow, but they also fell in love with the whole concept of Island Lake and the camaraderie that occurs amongst strangers in this magical place. Staff and guests often greet each other like old friends—because they are. A marketing person may use the term "brand advocate" to describe many of the enthusiastic Island Lake guests, but a better description would be "old friends bound by a love of mountain culture and the backcountry."

Island Lake has also been fortunate enough to have many creative characters amongst its staff, who are an essential ingredient to providing an enthralling experience. Many of the guides have been working for a decade or more—they know the terrain inside out and can spin a gripping yarn. They have also watched the full development of everything in this book. This includes the industry-changing transition from skinny skis to big fat skis (I must admit that powder photos looked deeper and more enveloping with the old skinny skis—but after having skied ridiculously deep powder, I understand the progression).

Several past and present Island Lake chefs contributed to Keith Liggett's award-winning *Island Lake Lodge: The Cookbook*, which came out in 2008. The 180-page volume featured a host of favourite recipes from over the years and the stunning photography of Henry Georgi. It follows the Island Lake food philosophy of French-inspired Rocky Mountain cuisine, with an effort to get as much produce and protein from as close to the lodge as possible.

There are also many dedicated characters working behind the scenes who make the entire operation run. No staff member should be overlooked. The logistics of running a backcountry lodge are intense, and there are many staff that work in the background to make it all happen. They may not get all the glory but they are an integral part of keeping the Island Lake experience in gear.

Dan McDonald and Family

The one thing everyone agrees on is that Dan had the original vision of catskiing at Island Lake. He worked incredibly hard with his partners to make it all happen. His wife Susan, daughter Jennie and son Parker were there as well, doing what ever needed to be done around the lodge. The family atmosphere was an integral part of the Lodge experience in those first winters. Dan saw the value of media exposure early on and used it to the full potential. It cannot be understated how important this was in bringing Island Lake to the world.

"Island Lake always brought out the best and the worst in people. It is such a powerful piece of land. People that got near it became very possessive of it and at times very aggressive. I know it controlled a large portion of my productive life. I had many days of joy and a few days of sorrow. It was there that I learned to ski deep powder but never had enough time to really enjoy it. I was always working. I would say the same with Dale Bowman. What a workhorse he was and what a man. I really admire his stamina and dedication to making it work. All in all the project was a collaboration of many talented people and still is today."
– Dan McDonald; Island Lake visionary and Founder

"We moved to Elk Valley area in 1973 and raised our children there. One thing we often did with the kids was take them on picnics in the bush. We always enjoyed finding new spots as we searched for huckleberries each summer and eyed the hills for elk.

Dan and his buddies snowmobiled and ski toured around Fernie through the 1980s. While doing this, they formulated the idea of building a cabin in the mountains. This would be an ideal convenience for all their four seasons' adventures in the mountains.

Soon this idea escalated to developing a business where they would escort people to this cabin and offer to guide them snowmobiling, ski touring, or cross country skiing – whatever they wanted. They dubbed this 'High Country Adventures.' After pinning a name to their plan they began to seek out the feasibility of such a venture, and especially, where they could place their little cabin in the wild.

Back to picnics with the family: in October of 1986 we took our little family, went up to Island Lake, and had a picnic on the beach area there, which looks much the same as it does today. I recall how we admired a huge full moon over the lake with the backdrop of the Lizard Range. One of those pictures of a lifetime, branding the mind.

I said to my husband, 'Why don't you build your cabin here?'

He replied, 'We'd never get permission, this is private land.'

I said, 'Wouldn't hurt to ask, this is perfect and there's even a road back to town.'

That winter they did inquire, got permission and by the next spring Island Lake Lodge was on its way.

From that time forward, for the next six or seven years, our life was to change drastically. Things became intensely busy as we continued to run our industrial construction company while we threw ourselves into the Lodge.

Family picnics continued. Every one of them was on the site of the Lodge. First it was at the building site. I packed coolers and coolers full of food up there for our family and the wonderful circle of friends that pitched in all they could to give us a hand.

Island Lake Lodge was first built with the idea of offering ski touring and cross-country skiing. We had purchased a small snowcat to ferry goods and people in. Soon we stepped up to a slightly bigger snowcat, and very soon after that we bought our first PistenBully. By then the focus swung to featuring snowcat skiing.

Dan McDonald at the helm. *Photo: Henry Georgi*

The Lodge brought some very intriguing people into our lives. There were guides and aspiring guides coming to our home for interviews, and later, discussions about the business. Also, skiers and snowboarders who were currently the stars of the latest snow movies and pictured in the magazines. The children became relaxed and even friends with some of these, foremost, Craig Kelly and Scot Schmidt. As well, there were photographers such as Mark Gallup and Henry Georgi who followed the business from the start and really contributed to putting us on the map with the media.

Craig was especially fond of both Parker and Jennie and helped them get 'sponsored' by Burton. All through their teen years, we received boxes of goods—from snowboards to every item of snow clothing one can imagine.

But I don't think any of that stuff meant as much to my children as the personal friendship Craig offered them. Parker has a memorable photo of being carried on Craig's shoulders—it looks like an older brother with his sibling. Jennie has cherished memories of trips with Craig Kelly as well as personal letters of encouragement from him.

When bringing people in on the snowcat for the first time, I recall telling them that 'we will emerge from this cedar forest to one of the most spectacular views you'll have ever seen,' and each time as we swung into the

parking area and they were awed by what they saw, it brought tears to my eyes. I do not recall anyone ever being disappointed with that view of Island Lake."
– Susan McDonald

"I've seen it all with the lodges, the struggles, the fights, the failures, the glory, the beauty of the place. Sometimes it could bring peace and love, sometimes bitterness.

It is a place for me where friendships were found and lost. Just ask any wife or child of a mountain guide: the dad is gone to work a lot. The place was built on sweat and tears, not too much blood.

It was really neat meeting Craig Kelly. As a young girl, I wasn't into ballet or girly stuff, so when my younger brother and I and our friends saw Craig and the guys snowboard—it was so amazing. Soon we converted from skiing to snowboarding. All the descriptions of his style are true, but what people may not know is he was super to us kids, he was down-to-earth, funny and kind . He always left his ego at the door, you could say. We didn't really realize he was famous because he was so nice. Looking back it was pretty neat to have that experience. Sometimes he would give us stickers or a shirt; that was like gold. Craig, Scot Schmidt and Mark Gallup made Island Lake famous; it was mostly never heard of before that.

The winter was my favourite time at the Lodge. The Bear Lodge had the smell of a wood fire, diesel of the snowcat, ski wax, and there was always a warm feeling, especially after an amazing ski day. Sometimes people partied too late and would almost miss the skiing. In the kitchen, Chef Alain always had delicious and amazing meals, the smell of fresh baking in the A.M. was wonderful."
- Jennie McDonald Krynski

Henry Georgi

Like many others, Henry came to Fernie to ski. He was a budding photographer at the time and came up to the Lodge in the early '90s. His shots from Island Lake were soon getting published and he became a regular at the Lodge. Henry shot all the photos for the award-winning *Island Lake Lodge: the Cookbook* and still resides in Fernie B.C.

"I first met Dan McDonald at the Toronto Ski show and he invited me out. When I first showed up at Island Lake, there was only one lodge. The rooms were upstairs, with anywhere from two to four beds per room. It was all pretty open as you could see from upstairs down to the main floor. There weren't many actual tours running. Dan brought Steve Kujit up to work with me (at the time I think he was driving cat, building roads for Island Lake part time). The only other group there was a film crew with the DesLauriers brothers. At that time there was Dan, Dale and Bob running things."
– Henry Georgi; Photographer

Reto Keller

The sweet smell of Captain Black pipe tobacco wafts through the forest; there's a thick Swiss yodel dancing through the air followed by a Santa Claus-esque chuckle. You picture a set of thumbs slipping under suspender straps followed by a quick check of the pipe between puffs, and that's exactly what is happening. But there is more: a big grin framed by a salt and pepper beard, and sunglasses—never goggles—topped off with a brimmed hat more suited for golfing than skiing. This is the trademark of Reto Keller, legendary Island Lake head guide.

In the evenings, just as guests pause between the gourmet dinner and dessert, a seemingly clumsy janitor with broom in hand bumps into everybody's chairs. Before they can look up and realize it's Reto, loud Swiss accordion music kicks in and Reto entertains the guests with vigorous stick on broom, playing with Jimi Hendrix behind-the-back moves, followed by equally enthusiastic wooden-spoon playing. Reto was also a mentor to several of the current Island Lake guides. This is the legend of Reto Keller, Swiss Guide.

Left: Reto Keller and Mark Gallup looking distinguished smoking pipes.

Jake Blattner

In the mid-1990s, Ride Snowboards was a heavy hitter in the industry. Second only to Burton, they had a cast of colourful characters and misfits that outshone all other teams. Jake's first visit was also with Jason Ford on that legendary Ride photo shoot in 1995. A seemingly quiet person who didn't waste his words, Jake was a powerhouse on the snowboard. If you wanted to hike a ridge, Jake was there. If there was a cliff to jump, Jake was there. If there was anything that seemed impossible, Jake was the first to try it. If you wanted to stay up all night, Jake was there. If you said his actions spoke for him, then there was a lot of shouting going on! Like Jason, Scot, Craig and Mark, Jake jumped on the opportunity to become a shareholder shortly after his first visit in 1995. When Scot came up with the idea of The Gathering Music Festival in 1996, Jake was ready to help out. The festival was an inspiration for Jake's contribution, known as the "Jam Sessions," that ran from 2001 to 2003. It was a snowboard camp in the late spring with a jam format. Snowboard jam during the day, and music jams in the evenings. Jake made a living as a professional snowboarder, but his bass playing is equally top notch. And like all bass players, Jake was in the background driving the tempo to all the fun things that came to Island Lake.

The Gallups

Mark and Beth Gallup played an integral role in the development and success that Island Lake has enjoyed. Featured throughout this book, Mark's photos were the catalyst for much of the media coverage produced. Mark was the first to bring the legendary skiers and snowboarders to the Lodge—a few of whom also became shareholders. Mark's wife Beth ran the whole operation, together with another shareholder, for a few years.

"Strangely—especially for those who know me—my favourite memories of Island Lake are at night. A spontaneous moonlight cat ride and ski with Reto Keller, a random collection of staff and a few guests who were still awake. Drinking a beer with Mike Thorton, watching him coax one of the original PistenBullies back to life before morning. Walking down out of Geisha Bowl in the light of Halley's Comet: a much calmer experience than the ride up on the back of Mark's single-seat sled. Standing out in the snow, watching it silently accumulate on the branches of the trees. Marvelling at the giant owl standing guard in late spring, when it was just me and the mice in the Red Eagle." – *Beth Gallup; Vice-President and Board Chair, 1996-2000*

Some of the industry shareholders after the purchase from Shell. L to R – Mark Gallup, Craig Kelly, Scot Schmidt, Jake Blattner and Jason Ford

Past industry shareholders in 2011. L to R – Mark Gallup, Scot Schmidt, Jake Blattner and Jason Ford.
Photo: Mike McPhee

Mark Gallup and Jake Blattner jam with journalist Mike Berard in the Bear Lodge. *Photo: Mike McPhee*

Steve Kuijt

Steve came to Fernie on the popular ski-bum program. Within a few short years his powder prowess was noticed and he was shooting photos at Island Lake with Mark Gallup and Henry Georgi. His moustached, powder-filled face was plastered on the first *Powder Magazine* covers of Island Lake. Soon after that he was working at the Lodge, driving cats and ski guiding. By 2005 he was the General Manager of the place. Steve is one of those natural storytellers who can enthrall you with a story from start to finish. His vast knowledge of the Island Lake property is second to none.

"The first year I was there we had guests, but not many, and lots of them were family and friends of Dan, Dale and Bob. Dan would invite almost anybody with a camera and a good story to come up and ski. Word of mouth from a few early guests like Doug Mills and Graham Phipps brought a few folks from Calgary for the first two years, and then somehow Dan got the Egan brothers to show up with a camera crew. At the same time I was shooting with Henry Georgi at the ski hill, and Dan let me bring him up to shoot stills.

In those days I was still a cat driver most of the time, but started guiding the media groups, as I had worked with several photographers away from Island Lake. I skied for two Warren Miller segments with Bill Heath at Lake Louise and at Snow Valley and met up with an old friend, Mark Gallup, who was shooting with them. Henry published lots of Island Lake photos, Mark got back-to-back covers in *Powder Magazine* and Island Lake came out in that year's Warren Miller film. The next year we were booked up and were looking to build a new lodge. I spent over 20 years skiing and hiking up there in the prime of my life, during a most exciting time in the development of the place. The stories could go on for a long time, as almost any day you spend at Island Lake has special experiences. The place is magic and is made for creating stories."

– Steve Kuijt; Island Lake Guide, Cat Driver and past General Manager.

Rick Emmerson

Rick has been with the company for 15 years and is currently the assistant guiding manager. Don't let Rick's soft-spoken, calm demeanour fool you; he can rip up the slopes with the best of them and also tells a good joke.

"I love feeding off of the energy of guests being exposed to the mountain environment; many times I have been told that the experience is life changing. The deepest day I have witnessed at Island Lake was 160 cms in 24 hrs. During that storm there were times that it snowed 10-15 cms per hour."

– Rick Emmerson; Assistant Guiding Manager

Steve Kloepzig and Candice Froneman

Big Steve, as he is known, has been guiding at Island Lake for 15 years now. His booming, gregarious voice and personality are hard to miss in the trees. Steve also spends the warm months glading terrain with Corrie. His wife, Candice, is also a powder skiing veteran and has been guiding at Island Lake for about 9 years. They have two lovely daughters and reside in Fernie.

"My best memories at the lake are tail gunning with the Captain (Corrie) and working for Craig Kelly and his 'troop 56 crew' (first time he brought up 12 friends). We had a couple of runs and it was sweet. We loaded up for another; I watched Craig sit down in the corner and he just kinda look over his crew. They were bursting at the seams, as it was as good as it gets. Then this huge smile came over his face as he looked at all his buddies and I knew then that it would be hard to ever leave Island Lake. I mean, if a world champ loved this place, then I have a dream job."

– Steve Kloepzig; Ski Guide

Right: "Big" Steve Kloepzig taking the guests a little higher above the Non-Stop drop on a beautiful day in the alpine. *Photo: Mike McPhee*

Jason Ford

Jason Ford first showed up on the scene in 1995. Ride Snowboards brought their entire team up to Island Lake for a photo shoot, and Jason was one of their top riders at the time. After that first visit you couldn't keep Jason away. Like Craig Kelly, he had been to Whistler for contests in the early '90s, and also like Craig's, his career was moving away from competition and into backcountry freeriding. One of the best technical and calculated riders of his time, Jason was always taking his riding to the next level, on steeper and more exposed lines.

His most famous line at Island Lake has never been repeated—and probably never should be. High on the Lizard Range is a very steep slope hanging above a 200-foot cliff. There is only one way up and one way down that involves a very exposed dogleg corner. If you don't make the corner, you go off the cliff. On his second turn from the knife-edge ridge top, the slope "sloughed heavily." There was no place to escape. Thinking quickly, he made an unorthodox surfer move—he duck dived and the rushing snow went over his head—a move that would only work on such steep terrain. The onlookers thought it was over for Jason as they watched the snow cascade off the 200-foot cliff. Seconds later, Jason popped up from the same spot and continued to ride down like nothing happened. The spot was later named "Duck Dive Dog Leg." A shareholder in the operation, Jason probably also wins the most-photos-ever-published award for his prolific talent in front of the camera and his very frequent visits.

"Mark and Craig were like brothers. They lived together, worked together, and travelled together. It seemed as if Craig was listening through the walls to see where Mark and I were planning our next adventure. Maybe it was his competitive nature? Regardless, it was fun to watch the two work together (or around each other) throughout the years. Just like brothers, I know they loved each other tremendously.

I would attribute Island Lake's success in the media to a few key factors, a) Gallup and his ability to bring in the pros to shoot in his private backcountry studio, b) the diversity of images that were captured there from the likes of Craig or the Ride Team, c) the family feeling that the Lodge and staff brought to the scene, and finally d) the terrain, which is simply breath-taking. There was something more that came from that little cabin, lake and the Lizard Range. Something I can't explain, but something that boils down an emotion that seems to get my world back on track."
– Jason Ford; Pro Snowboarder and past shareholder

Nick Morris

Nick's association with Island Lake started as a 15-year-old, when he spent a summer peeling the larch logs for what would become the Bear Lodge. A few years later he sporadically worked at the Lodge as a tail guide—like many of the other guides Reto Keller mentored and showed that being a ski guide could actually be a job. Doubling as a ski model, Nick has had many shots of himself published, including the cover of *Ski Canada*. Nick met his wife Cathy at the Lodge and they have two daughters (more girls, there must be something in the water) who are ski racers.

"I have many great memories from Island Lake and guided many of the media trips over the years. Guys like Trevor Petersen, Seth Morrison, Glen Plake, Kent Kreitler have all been part of the program. I have guided elsewhere and have to say that one of the reasons Island Lake stands out is because the ski terrain is so close to the Lodge. A 15-minute cat ride and you are into the goods."
– Nick Morris; Ski Guide

Jason Ford *Photo: Mike McPhee*

Corrie and Brenda Wright

Corrie is the longest working continual employee at Island Lake, with 20-plus years under his belt. He is one of those laid back, patient guys who takes just about everything in stride. Corrie's good nature is popular with guests and other staff alike. In summer, he wields a chainsaw, creating habitat for the powder rider. His wife, Brenda, has also been with Island Lake for about 17 years and is also a guide. They have two daughters who are bound to be powder skiers.

"The operation has gone from pioneering to a well-oiled machine. When I started, the guests were in the Bear Lodge, the guides' room was in the dirt basement, there were very few staff, and very little glading to speak of. It was a real frontier operation... an exciting time, lots of media, lots of action.

"Island Lake is a Powder Kingdom that the snow lords have created for us. It's private land so we could help shape the powder-riding habitat, and it is close to Fernie so we can have a family life. Over the years we have made many friendships with staff and guests through the camaraderie of the powder. Catskiing is always at a great pace and the cat doesn't mind when it's snowing 10cm an hour!" – *Corrie Wright; Ski Guide*

"I started at Island Lake in October 1994. It was just the Bear Lodge then and I was the server, hostess, bartender, food prep, dishwasher and housekeeper. I started guiding for Reto the next winter in 1995 and still love every minute working up here. I was involved from the start with the hiking and trail program as well. Where has the time gone? It seems like yesterday when I walked out of the Island Lake office with my dream job!" – *Brenda Wright; Ski Guide*

Dave Treadway

"Island Lake was where I went on my first trip as a pro skier. It was in 2005 with Eric Berger, and I was like a kid in a candy shop. I just couldn't believe how big my bed was! Thanks for hosting us skiers and treating us like royalty!"
– *Dave Treadway; Pro Skier*

Corrie and Brenda got married up in the terrain and then shredded some pow together... aaww. *Photo: Dave Silver*

Niki LePage

Niki has been guiding at Island Lake for 10 years and is currently the guiding manager. After spending time with her you can see why she has succeeded to the top of a male-oriented industry; her work ethic and perseverance are a great model for all. Blake, her canine companion, is an avalanche rescue dog and can be found looking for scratches and snacks around the Lodge.

"I am driven by wanting to share with guests my love for the mountains and powder skiing. My goal is to keep everyone safe and give guests the best guided ski experience of their life. I love catskiing because of the untouched powder and enjoying a particular area with only my group. Not to mention the warm comfortable rides up! People are also what make Island Lake special to me. Both my great coworkers and many guests have become good friends over the years."
– *Niki LePage; Guiding Manager*

Shin Campos

"I remember seeing Island Lake Lodge in the old *Transworld* magazines when Jason Ford and the Ride dudes were there a lot, Craig Kelly as well. I grew up near Nelson, B.C. in the Slocan Valley, so it was kinda close. The early days were great because it was a time before I had a snowmobile, so you spent lots of time just riding and coming across stuff you'd want to shoot. I remember lots of powder runs but then finding various cliff drops and chutes to ride. All those ridges that we'd hike to hit the chutes and drops were super cool."
– *Shin Campos; Pro Snowboarder*

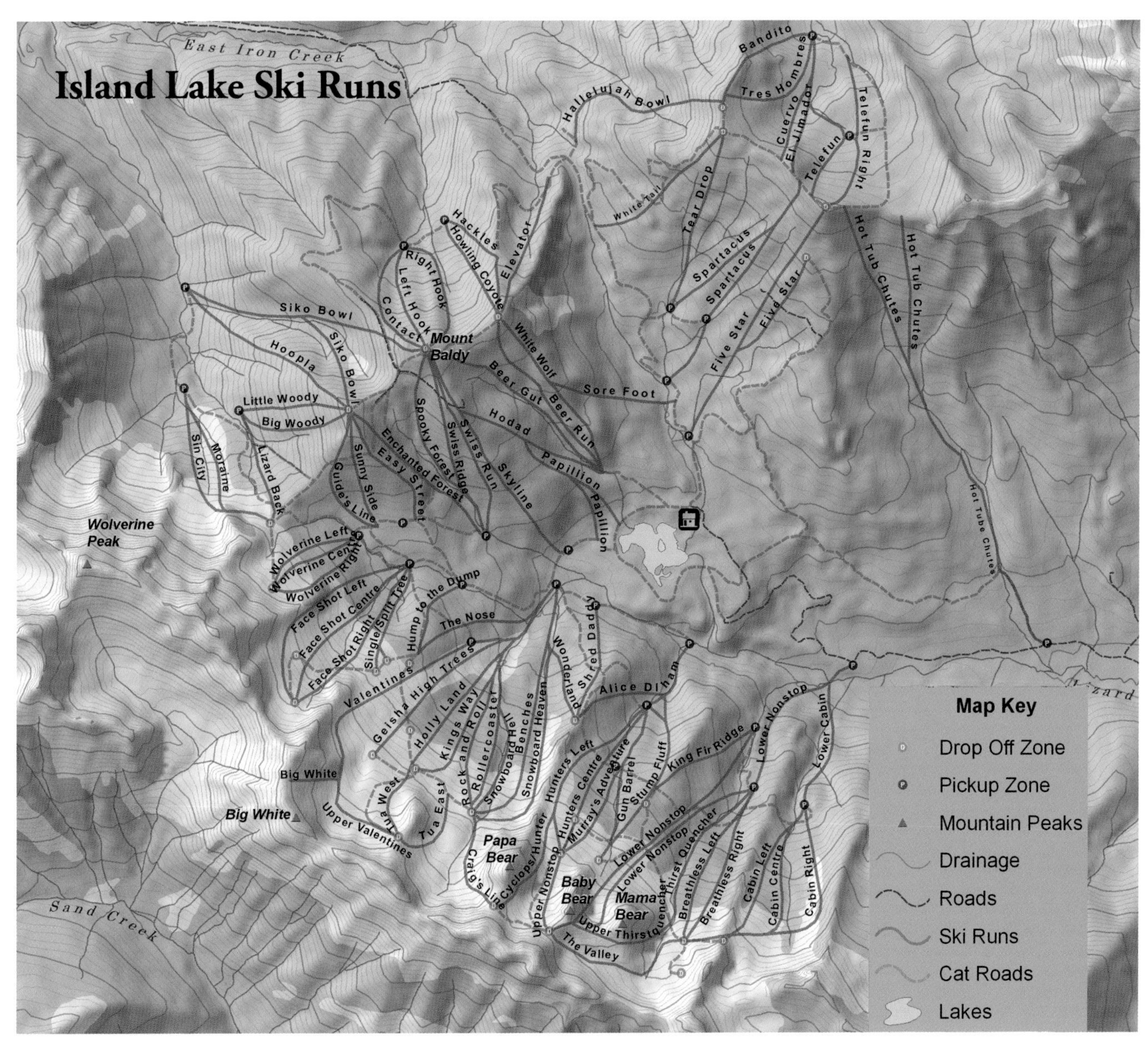

The Terrain

Some people cannot get enough tree skiing, while others are addicted to high alpine bowls and ridges. Luckily, Island Lake's 7,000 acres of terrain has a big helping of both.

Let's start up high. Behind each of the peaks of the Three Bears is a saddle and snowcat drop points: Tua Time, Cyclops and Upper Nonstop—the three highest drop points within the Island Lake terrain. The big alpine bowls are separated by a series of ridges and each ridge is full of chutes and features. So in one run you can experience wide open, high alpine and perfectly gladed trees. Mount Baldy sits in the middle of the Valley and has perfect tree skiing on all sides. Runs like Sunny Side, Elevator and The Enchanted Forest are favourites with skiers and snowboarders. On the north side of the Valley is a shoulder of Mount Fernie, which has front and backside ski terrain. The Hot Tub Chutes come down from here and are the longest runs at 3,500 feet of vertical.

The trees start off small in the subalpine and continue down to the Valley floor, where they can be the size of coastal old growth trees. Guests are always impressed by the amount of tree skiing available. After 20 years of glading and enhancing habitat for the powder rider, what remains is a legacy of perfectly spaced timber, which is excellent terrain for all of the snowy storm days that Island Lake is legendary for.

Circe Wallace adds to a great view of the upper alpine near Tua East. Papa Bear Peak is visible to the left and Cyclops beside in the notch. Duck Dive Dog Leg is just right of the notch. *Photo: Mark Gallup*

Scot Schmidt

Scot Schmidt is one of those quiet reserved guys who does not draw a lot of attention in a crowd. He tends to be the laid-back people-watcher in the corner. This is in contrast to the place he holds in the history of the snow industry and to many other professional athletes at his level. If you are a non-skier or if you happen to have been living in a cave for the last 25 years, Scot has the distinct industry title of "The Original Freeskier." He is recognized by most as being the first big mountain pro skier who managed to make a living jumping off stuff and shredding powder. Back in an age when ski company sponsorships revolved around alpine racers, ski ballet and moguls, Scot sought a different path and defined a niche that has since become the standard for pro ski athletes around the world. Part of his legacy was created and documented at Island Lake Lodge, where he became a shareholder, director and regular Lodge fixture.

Part of the path Scot carved in the early '90s was through his ski movie segments. At a time when household VCRs were exponentially increasing the reach of "Ski Porn," snow video stars were able to bring the "radness" right into your living room. This changed the game. Freeskiing pros had a medium, locations became household names and filmmakers could make some money. After filming several movies with Warren Miller, Scot hooked up with a young upstart filmmaker with a unique perspective on the world. Greg Stump captured Scot's effortless big mountain style, added cutting-edge music—all while following a more "interesting" plot-line than the average ski movie. Scot's laid back, friendly style not only looked good on film but probably contributed to why he has been on The North Face ski team for 30 years now. In an industry full of egos, short careers and overhype, Scot is still skiing 100 days a season and not taking himself too seriously.

Scot was the key person who started the summer Gathering Music Festival that ran annually at Island Lake from 1996-2000. The Gathering, as it was known,

The Bear Lodge fireplace has witnessed a lot of lounging, as Scot Schmidt is here after a day on the slopes. *Photo: Mike McPhee*

A more recent shot of Scot and Papa Bear Peak.
Photo: Aaron Whitfield

was a classic multi-day folk music and wilderness festival. Though the event is no longer running, it is still talked about with reverence and it is a part of the Island Lake mystique.

Scot is still a regular at the Lodge and comes a few times a season. It is most likely that he has skied more days at Island Lake than anyone other than some of the long-term ski guides. He can still be found relaxing by the river rock fireplace in the Bear Lodge after a good day on the slopes, quietly contemplating and taking in the après scene.

"Scot showed skiers that a living could be made from skiing while staying true to the spirit of skiing... not competition. He showed skiers that brands and film companies should pay you for your talent, and not just in free trips. He was a businessman who understood that athletes hold value. No one would watch a ski film if there were no pro skiers, so they should get compensated accordingly. He also was the antithesis to the Glen Plake model of pro skier, which was more focused on image and attitude. Decades later, it's hard to say which model is more prevalent, but I like to think that Schmidt's quiet confidence and humility still inspires skiers." – *Mike Berard; Editor of Coast Mountain Culture*

"Scot definitely pioneered the role of pro freeride skier in North America; he basically helped create the career I have. He also opened the North American industry's eye to the potential of freeriding, plus he is a total shredder and pushed the progression and style of the sport." – *Eric Hjorleifson; Pro Skier*

"Scott was a huge part of starting the freeskiing movement in the '90s and was basically the man to watch during that time... I loved watching his pow segments from the Greg Stump movies!" – *Ian McIntosh; pro skier*

"I think Scot was the Kelly Slater or Shawn White of his day... His style was the main thing that impacted the industry and it's still alive in a few skiers today. Proper style indeed." – *Eric Crosland, Sherpas Cinema*

In his own words:

"Our goal with the Greg Stump film *Siberia*, which also came through in *P-Tex, Lies,* was to inspire skiers and boarders to coexist, as did Craig Kelly and I. It's more about the character of the individual than what they ride. It's important for ski and snowboard culture to have something in common, because we share the same mountains and the same passions.

Snowboarding definitely brought new energy in, and continues to add and shape the sport. Skiing and snowboarding together make up our industry. It was never an issue between Craig and me which tools we used; we just enjoyed the ride." – *Scot Schmidt*

An iconic Island Lake landmark complete with an iconic skier. Scot Schmidt is a reminder to us all of where our freeriding roots have come from. The catch phrase "Extreme skier" has always followed Scot's career, but he was the master of steep terrain and skied everything with no effort, reading the natural terrain like a porpoise in a wave; smooth isn't a strong enough word! *Photo Mark Gallup*

Scot Schmidt

The classic, effortless style of Scot Schmidt. *Photo: Mark Gallup*

Cover Stories

Cover shots are the pinnacle of success for most photographers, athletes and locations. They represent the apex of attainable print media hype. Athletes with a photo retainer contract make more money off the prized cover. A high profile cover can do wonders for a photographer, furthering their career and solidifying their reputation. A cover shot can give a specific location or operation a boost in profile that marketing dollars simply can't buy. As you can imagine, industry politics can also come into play. Why did such and such an athlete get three covers in said magazine this year? Why is there an energy drink logo visible? Cover photos are worth their weight in gold. This is proven by stories of advertising blackmail and intense brand pressure on editors and magazine staff. Hence, there is often more involved than a great photograph, especially in recent years with major corporations sponsoring athletes and spending vast amounts of money to connect with today's youth.

While rummaging through the archives, I was astonished at how many cover shots have been produced at Island Lake over the last couple of decades. A good cross section of international print media is covered. Mark Gallup has the lion's share, as he was a regular fixture and shareholder at the Lodge for many years. His position as Senior Photographer at *Transworld Snowboarding* for a solid decade helped as well. An eclectic mix of magazines have reproduced the Island Lake aesthetic and each cover photo adds a little more to the colourful history of this little lodge in the Lizard Range of the Rocky Mountains. The following is a selection of the magazines we could find copies of; though, we suspect there are a few others out there.

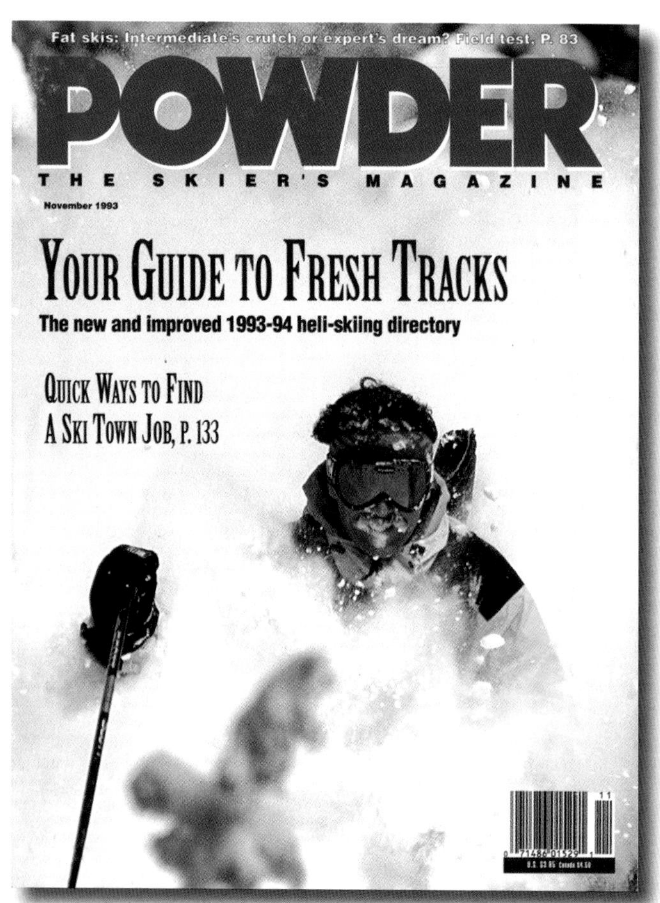

Steve Kuijt did it all at Island Lake: Cat driver, Guide, General Manager and ski model. *Photo: Mark Gallup*

Craig displays some classic style yet again. *Photo: Mark Gallup*

Christy Wiserman. *Photo: Mark Gallup*

Jake Blattner bags an early *Transworld* cover.
Photo: Jeff Curtes

Dale Rehberg on the cover of a classic Ride catalogue.
Photo: Mark Gallup

Neil Mason in the trees. *Photo: Mark Gallup*

East Coast rider Ian Spiro samples Island Lake.
Photo: Jeff Curtes

Dave Heath. *Photo: Mark Gallup*

Eric Pehota on the cover, with a Trevor Petersen tribute inside.
Photo: Mark Gallup

Sean O'Brien. *Photo Mark Gallup*

Chris Swierz. *Photo: Mark Gallup*

Craig is at it again with his snow surfing. *Photo: Mark Gallup*

Paul Nelson. *Photo: Mark Gallup*

Shin Campos on the cover of the annual interview issue. The whole article was shot at Island Lake. *Photo: Mark Gallup*

Matt Goodman. *Photo: Mark Gallup*

Paul Nelson. *Photo: Mark Gallup*

Mike Orr. *Photo: Mark Gallup*

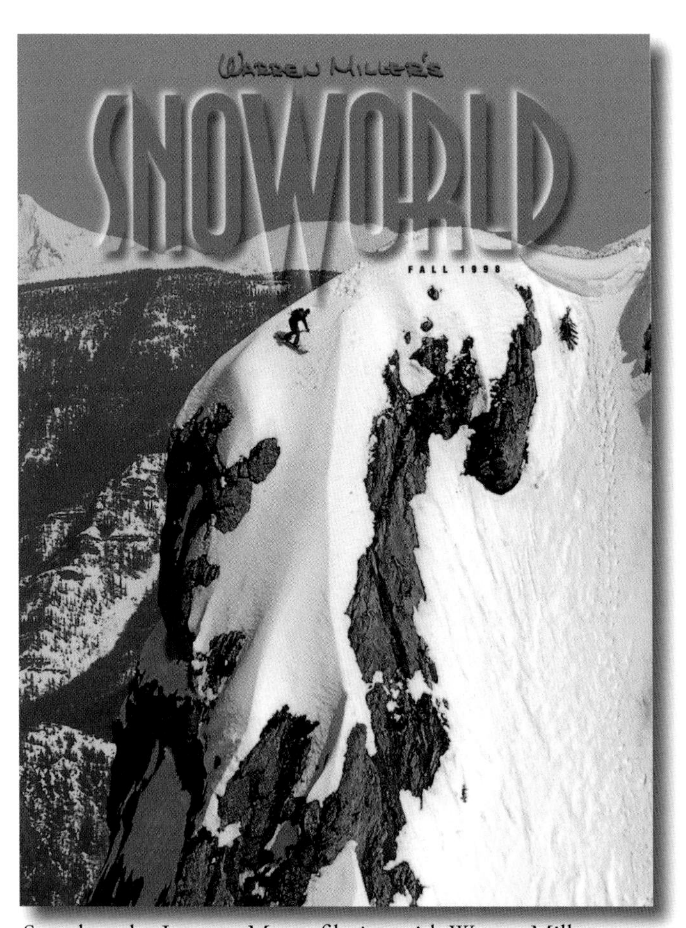

Snowboarder Jonaven Moore filming with Warren Miller.

Chris Swierz. *Photo: Mark Gallup*

Victoria Jealouse in some sweet powder and light.
Photo: Mark Gallup

Aleksi Litovaara on the cover of Helly Hansen's *Alive* magazine.
Photo: Mark Gallup

Long-term guide and Fernie local Nick Morris shredding the Cyclops. *Photo: Mark Gallup*

Victoria Jealouse circa 1998. *Photo: Mark Gallup*

Rube Goldberg gets the cover. *Photo: Dano Pendygrasse*

Chris Booth drinking the Island Lake Kool-Aid.
Photo: Tony Harrington

Mica Heliskiing Marketing Director, Darryn Shewchuck.
Photo: Dave Silver

Silver Screen

Over the years a fair bit of celluloid film and tape have been shot at Island Lake. The Lizard Range has attracted the full gamut of moviemakers and TV producers with its dramatic peaks, chute-filled ridgelines and deep powder. Cinematic alumni includes: Greg Stump, Warren Miller, the Egan Brothers, Teton Gravity Research, Sherpas Cinema and Matchstick Productions. Island Lake Lodge starred in various TV shows such as: *The Ride Guide*, *Ski TV*, *Pleasure De Ski*, *The White Room Episodes*, *Canada AM* and even an episode of *Man vs Wild* with Bear Grylls.

In 2010 Sherpas Cinema filmed a large portion of their multi-award-winning feature-length movie *ALL.I.CAN* at Island Lake and sister company Mica Heliskiing. This kind of exposure is invaluable to the success of an operation and adds a rich layer to the legacy of Island Lake. In the early '90s Greg Stump was busy bringing a new narrative to the bourgeoning genre of ski and snowboard movies. He incorporated an often zany, off-the-wall plot line with arty camera work and editing; then he added in an equally interesting sound track. Incorporating ski and snowboard culture together was also a new concept. At the time it was nothing less than groundbreaking. The fact that Scot Schmidt, Glen Plake and Craig Kelly were regular characters in the powder-filled, controlled chaos added legitimacy to the works. Stump's 1994 *P-Tex, Lies and Duct Tape* proved a pivotal moment in ski movie-making and solidified Island Lake as a premier snow media destination. The long segment at the end of the movie showed skiers and snowboarders not only coexisting but thriving together in backcountry. The heli shots of the terrain and Lodge are stunning footage, even in today's standards. The snippets of interviews with legends Scot and Craig speak to a transitional time in the snow industry. The all around accolades and great shots made the Lodge's phones ring off the hook and were certainly worth their weight in promotional gold.

"Stumpy's films changed the landscape of action sports at the time — he was really creative, I think Island Lake gave him the environment to do what he was imagining in his mind."
– *Eric Crosland; Sherpas Cinema.*

"Greg Stump elevated ski filmmaking from simple travelogue and resort-based profiles to a true storytelling medium. Actually, you could probably say Stump brought ski filmmaking back to what it was originally, and shed light on the people who make skiing so interesting as a lifestyle and culture. He also appreciated the role of music in ski films more than anyone else, and could arguably be credited with forming the modern action sports format of killer music matched to segments."
– *Mike Berard; Editor of Coast Mountain Culture*

Right: The cover for *P-Tex, Lies and Duct Tape* with Scot and the now famous tree on Spineback Ridge.
Photo: Mark Gallup. Video box design: Ace Mackay-Smith

Scot Schmidt and Craig Kelly's inspired campaign to bring ski and snowboard culture together was also well documented in *P-Tex, Lies and Duct Tape* as well as another Stump movie *Siberia*.

"Scot and Craig were the kings then, and to have them both there in the same film was amazing. Craig Kelly was a gem to work with... very smart, well read and, oh yeah, he could snowboard pretty well. I miss him very much... Island Lake was one of those epicentres that was blooming. It was an honour to have been there in the early days. It was such a great, quiet place and killer powder — some of the best snow I had skied."
– *Greg Stump; Film Producer*

"Shooting the Warren Miller movie *Ride* was the first time I ever met Craig, and being pretty young I was pretty stoked to say the least. It was just two young guys riding and filming with Craig in his own backyard. Amazing! I also got to go on another early trip for a Burton team shoot at Island Lake. It was the first place I met Bryan Iguchi, too. He's another one of snowboarding's most well-rounded characters. Island Lake holds most of its memories for me in the collection of amazing people that were all drawn there and that I got the good fortune to meet along the way."
– *Jonaven Moore; Pro Snowboarder*

Filming the Warren Miller movie *Ride*

The segment of Seth Morrison pounding through over-the-head blower pow in MSP's 1996 movie *Fetish* was some of the deepest snow anyone had seen on film at the time. The image of Seth without a hat, with just his flying hair visible through the powder cloud is one of those moments that was seared into many a skier's brain.

In 2002 Teton Gravity Research brought a young Travis Rice, Micah Black and Scot Schmidt to film a segment for their movie *The Prophecy*. This movie again highlighted skiers and snowboarders coexisting in the backcountry.

In more recent years, ski and snowboard videos have become a bit more common and formula based. Edit in a jib segment followed by Alaska segment, followed by obligatory powder helmet-cam segment, add energy drink logo and über-cool beats. Video cameras and consumer editing programs have become commonplace and the Internet has provided the ultimate platform for getting your brand message out or just showcasing your mountain vacation video.

In a desire to create something different, Island Lake and sister company Mica Heli Skiing partnered with Sherpas Cinema to develop a half hour TV show *The Balance of Powder*, as well as create footage for the Sherpas' two-year project *ALL.I.CAN*. The full-length movie *ALL.I.CAN* has gone on to win awards at just about every film festival around, including Best Feature Length Movie at the Banff Mountain Film Festival, Movie of the Year at the Powder Video Awards and ESPN has called it the "Best Ski Movie Ever."

The Sherpas brought their original aesthetic and cinematic wizardry to Island Lake and Mica Heliskiing, creating some of the most stunning footage ever shot at either location. At Island Lake, a 300-foot wirecam cable was set up for a group powder shot through the trees. Even though it took about 200 man-hours for a few seconds of video, the perspective of the camera following the skiers through the landscape is truly surreal. A high-speed camera was utilized for some 1,200 frame-per-second powder shots.

The Sherpas also brought their unique style of seasonal time lapses, where the scene goes from summer to fall to winter and then has a skier come through the frame. They made four visits or so in the winter of 2010/11; it was storming every time and the alpine was inaccessible, due to obscene amounts of snow. Even though some great powder shots were captured, the Island Lake alpine eluded the filmmakers. Regardless, as Greg Stump had in the '90s, the Sherpas used Island Lake as a blank white canvas and created something unique.

"The Sherpas changed ski cinematography forever, and to be honest, probably every kind of action sports media. *All.I.CAN.* is the most creative, smart ski film ever made, and there's a strong argument that it is the best. These guys have shown filmmakers that it is OK to take chances, try new things, and to be smart—a quality that is sadly missing from almost all action sports films. At best, action sports enthusiasts are shown as single-minded, obsessive outdoorsmen. The Sherpas have shown that anyone can be a skier and still be a caring, engaged human within the greater world. And while that might seem grandiose in the day-to-day scheme of things, it's nothing less than groundbreaking for the action sports film genre and our community in general."
– Mike Berard; Editor of Coast Mountain Culture

Dave Mossop from Sherpas Cinema shooting Ian McIntosh from the 350 foot long wirecam. *Photo: Mike McPhee*

"In the early '90s The Toronto Ski Show featured my live narrated ski film and after one of the shows the original owner of the Island Lake Lodge, Dan McDonald, came up and introduced himself to me. My first full-length film *The Extreme Dream* was filmed at Island Lake Lodge and my brother John and I skied the famed, Kitchen Wall via heli access. The place was paradise, family owned, a work in progress built on sweat and passion. Great food, fun evenings and deep, deep snow in the trees.

The location and the people make it. Today every backcountry outfit wants to sell the remote side of adventure. Island Lake was the real deal then as it is now. Authenticity, can't be recreated, it has to come from the passion of the people and the beauty of the place.

Craig Kelly was the bridge to bring ski and snowboard together; he lived the lifestyle and rode his board not to outdo skiers, but to join us in the mountains and experience them together. It was at Island Lake that I met him, and from there I only saw one culture, winter people, and that inspired our film *Return of the Shred-I,* where every one in the film had to ski and snowboard.

I've been lucky enough to ski all around the world, and I have seen more resorts and ski outfitters than most people can name. Island Lake lodge is always on my top ten locations to ski and ride when people ask me of my favourite location on this planet. Keep up the good work."

– Dan Egan; Pro Skier, Filmmaker and TV Host

Sherpa Cinema director and cinematographer Eric Crosland happy in the zone. Keeping cameras dry is always a mission on stormy days. *Photo: Mike McPhee*

Eric Hjorleifson and Matty Richard heading to the cat on a snowy morning ready for a day of filming.
Photo: Mike McPhee

Dave Mossop analysis the shot. *Photo: Mike McPhee*

Pro skier Ian McIntosh spent lots of time visiting Fernie while growing up—long-time Island Lake guide Nick Morris is his cousin. Here he is blasting through some trees on a stormy day for the Sherpas cameras.
Photo: Mike McPhee

The Fifth Element by Mark Gallup

The Fifth Element was the working title of a photography project exploring the contrast between summer and winter in the alpine zones of Island Lake. The results are no big surprise at first glance. Obviously, one has a hell of a lot a snow in it and the other one doesn't! With a second look you realize how much the snow changes the landscape: seemingly impossible lines of vertical rock are tamed by massive volumes of snow. Snow that fell quietly and mostly unnoticed, one small flake at a time, created ramps, drifts and chutes. Sooner or later these snowy features catch the eye of a winter visitor we know as the "Powder Junkie."

When this photo project was born, it was about the introduction of the human element into this vast landscape of four elements: wind, water, earth and fire. Fire made the rock. Rock broke down into earth. Wind and water and snow were the sculptors. When all these elements come together in perfect powdery harmony, the fun seeker—the fifth element—stands on top ready to drop in. Most fifth elements will ride, slash, yelp and carve their way to the bottom without realizing the miracle that just occurred. Although gravity whisks them away and their visit seems all too brief, for a moment they were a part of something that dates back to the making of Earth itself. Wrap your noodle around that one for a second.

Hopefully, at this point of the story you are scratching your chin and saying "Hmmmmmm" a lot. So let's talk about the Chinese for a second. The Elements differ in Chinese Astrology. The Chinese take out the element "air" and replace it with "wood" and "metal"—which is exactly what brings us to our powder paradise (besides the snowcat, of course). Yes, your skis and your snowboard are the reason you pursue this passion, and the Chinese knew it thousands of years ago. The Chinese also turn the elements into descriptions of the types of people that stand on top of snowy peaks.

Metal: The metal person is rigid and resolute in expression and intense with strong feelings.

Water: The water person is a good communicator and persuader, intuitive and sympathetic to others and good at conveying feelings and emotions.

Wood: The wood person has high morals, is self confident, expansive and co-operative, with wide and varied interests.

Fire: The fire person has leadership qualities, and is decisive, self confident, positive and assertive.

Earth: The earth person is serious, logical and methodical, intelligent, objective and good at planning. Earth represents the change of seasons.

So whether you're rigid, a persuader, co-operative, decisive or a good planner, these images are about how you, the fifth element, fit into the big picture because there is more going on than meets the eye.

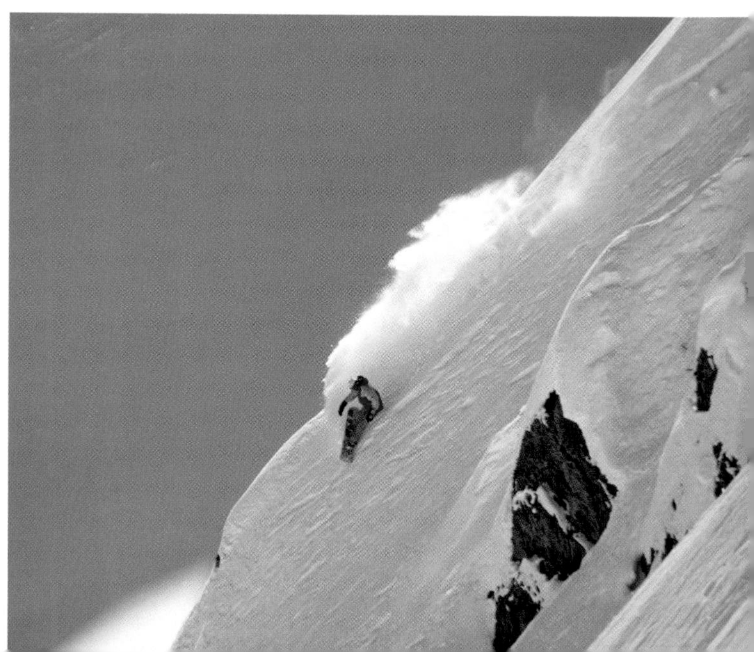

Emanual Krebs with style over the wind lip.

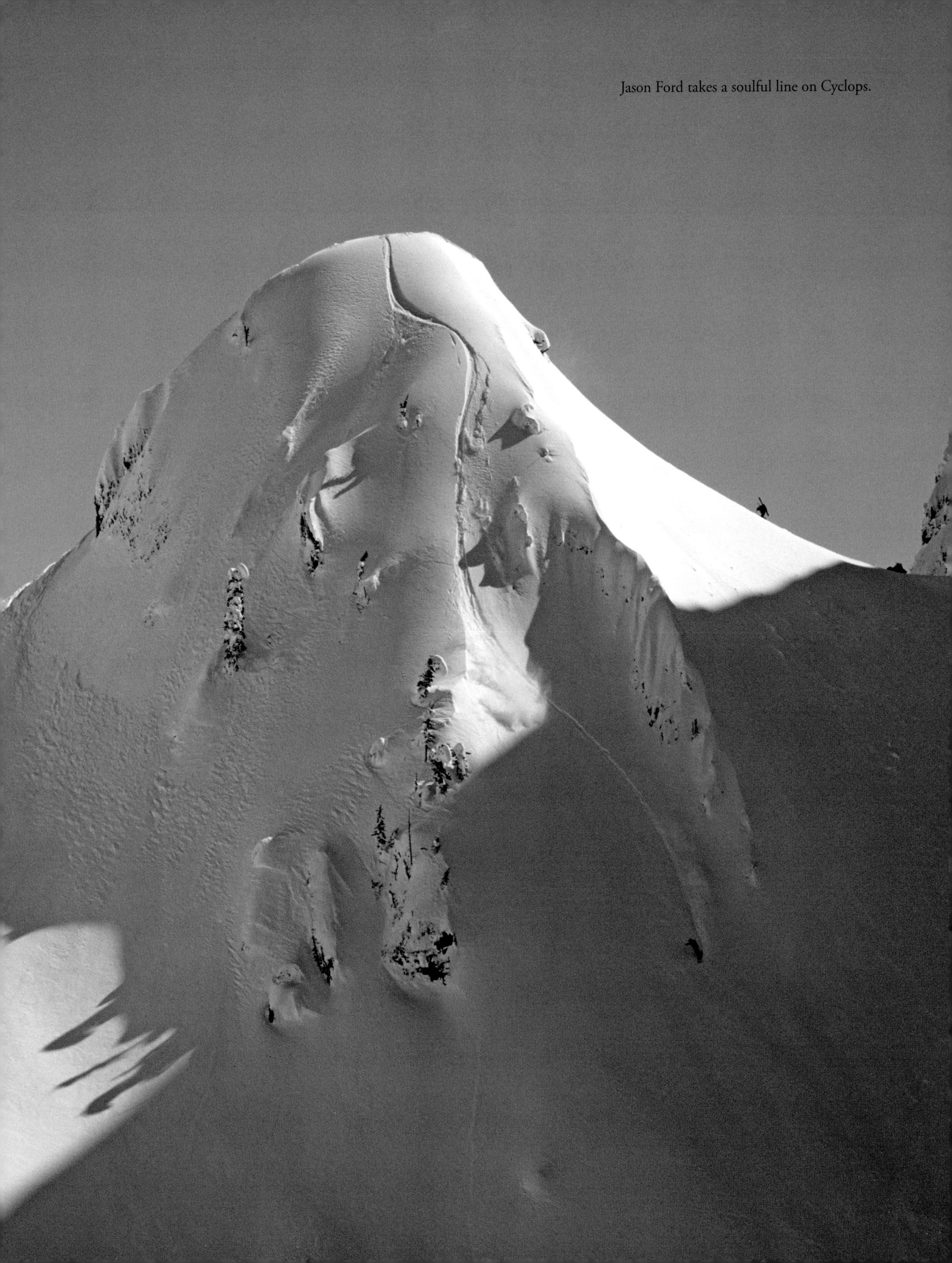

Jason Ford takes a soulful line on Cyclops.

Craig Kelly doing what he was meant to do—creating art on a white canvas.

Jason Ford on the infamous line Duck Dive, Dog Leg. Though not visible in this frame, Jason was hit by a sluff slide near the top and almost lost it... He ducked down like a surfer and let the snow go over.

A Rare Place for Wild Experiences by Lee-Ann Walker

Skiing at Island Lake is unlike anywhere else in the Rocky Mountains. Deep, dry snow accumulates into layers higher than a house. Feet stay warm enough to actually feel the steep descent. Skin is plumped up by humidity instead of exfoliated by wind-blasting, horizontal ice crystals. Dress code is layers, shed with exertion as the average winter temperature hovers around -8 Celsius. Dodging rocks — what rocks? Greeting you the at bottom of the ski slope are giant Western red cedars and hemlocks, reverently guarding wild secrets of the Cedar Valley.

In the winter, tracks, scat, rubbings and ghostlike apparitions tell clandestine stories in the snow. But why so much snow at Island Lake, and not 30 kilometres north up the Elk Valley? Nestled in this basin, high vertical snow towers push up warm, moist Pacific air tracking northeast. As it rises and cools it precipitates powder snow. Further east Arctic cold dry air masses dominate the prairie flatland. Here Pacific and Arctic air stall and mix overhead creating famous Fernie coldsmoke.

Along the skyline to the west, three bears and wolverine are not only the names of carnivores travelling up the Cedar Valley wildlife corridor en route to the Bull River or points north. They are also craggy peaks that are the result of infinite heat, pressure and time, transforming once limy grey ocean sediments into solid limestone. Horizontal layers telescoped eastward as the colliding Pacific plate moved under the North American plate, folding, faulting and thrusting the Earth's crust into frozen rock waves breaking toward the prairies. In the process, these sheets of ancient limestone sediments were shoved skyward over younger valley shale, sandstone and conglomerates. Once towering thousands of metres higher, the mountains have been affected by gravity, the elements, time and glaciers, which have carved away the landscape, depositing boulders and steepening valley slopes for skiing.

Nearly vertical limestone peaks transition to more friendly slopes but skiers beware of the sinkholes. Strangely limestone precipitated out of warm water but it dissolves in cold water. Swiss-cheese-like karst formations, softened by underwater rivers and surface melt water, create depressions — looking like cauldrons —that can trap unsuspecting skiers mid slope.

As skiers descend, they could pass over hibernating bears in deep slumber. Fortunately there is little chance of encountering sleeping *Ursus*, because like skiers, grizzly bears desire deep snow. In late fall, they seek out a cave, root ball or fallen log to dig under or a burned out tree stump to crawl inside, These natural features will then be protected by the snow insulation.

Snug as a bear on a rug, baby cubs, the size of a pound

The Cedar Valley narrow gauge railway.
Photo: Courtesy of the Fernie Museum

Turn of the century Cedar Valley logging camp.
Photo: Courtesy of the Fernie Museum

of butter, are born in mid winter. Cuddling her young, the grizzly sow will come out with multiple fur balls in May, long after the male bears have moved into the valley bottom forests along the creeks and Elk River. The Cedar Valley is prime habitat for bears — spring slopes smell of winter-kill, lush springtime vegetation in the valley bottom, summer berries, alpine roots and plants. On top, there is abundant wild space. Clearly people are not the only animals that love Island Lake.

Each spring the deep snowpack melts, recharging the soils, ground water and Lizard Creek, resulting in vegetation typical of the lush coastal rainforest. Towering cedars and plentiful plants filter the water, providing important rearing habitat for Westslope cutthroat trout populations that feed the main stem of the Elk River.

The cedar is the oldest living thing in the Valley, having survived fire, avalanches, disease and the destructive hand of man, and it is a unique tree to the Southern Rockies. The nearest stand of mature trees of this kind is hundreds of kilometres to the west near Yahk and St. Mary's Alpine Provincial Park. Over the past millennium, cedars have witnessed the changes that created this rare recreational resource. If these sentinel giants could tell you a story, they might tell a tale or two.

The first people to this forest, some 10,000 years ago, were the Ktunxa, who likely came seasonally to gather wild foods, medicine and supplies. Some desired the inner bark of the devil's club — when dried and ground, it could be made into powerful medicine. Young men certainly took cedar wood for crafting arrows, as it is light, easy to work with and straight-grained. Experienced craftsmen collected Western yew, a prized bow wood.

In 1873, Michael Phillips and John Collins explored this Valley prospecting for gold. No geological riches were discovered, but what they noted were "little green lizards" sunning themselves on a snow slide at the head of the Valley. They named the creek after the native long-toed salamander. Early wealth from this Valley came from the A1 graded cedar, fir and spruce, which was milled and shipped to build the settling turn-of-the-century prairie towns.

Perfect moose habitat in Island Lake. *Photo: Mike McPhee*

The 1907 sawdust pile half way up the Valley is all that remains of the North American Land and Lumber Company. On the cat ride up Cedar Valley, the road partially follows the abandoned grade used by a steam locomotive on a narrow gauge railway. With intensive logging and fires that reduced the timber supply, and with a train with a history of being off the rails more than on, logging ceased by the mid-1920s, and the rails were salvaged.

Moon setting on the Lizard Range, as seen from Fernie. *Photo: Henry Georgi*

While skiing look for notches lower on the stumps where men stood on elevated springboards opposite each other, pulling a crosscut saw. It is inconceivable the task of early loggers using horses to winter skid these unwieldy plants to the rail line.

In 1908, the Great Fernie Fire started from an unattended burn pile at the base of the Valley where it intersects with present day Highway 3 — formerly the Great Northern Railway line. The burn pile whipped up by hot August winds resulted in a firestorm that burned part of Cedar Valley, the city of Fernie and eastward toward the Alberta border. In 1931, a terrifying déjà vu jolted West Fernie residents into fearing another apocalypse, when a fire from Sand Creek jumped over the Lizard Range, burning upper Cedar Valley again, across Cabin Pass. Scorched trees throughout the valley remind us of this fiery past.

With a rich natural and human history, Island Lake Lodge, nestled in the Cedar Valley, is a rare place for never ending wild experiences.

Lee-Ann Walker has been a local naturalist since 1983, with an MA in Environment and Management and a BA in Heritage Interpretation.

Cutthroat Trout. *Photo: Mike McPhee*

Grizzly Bear. *Photo: Mike McPhee*

Old Growth Western Red Cedar Tree. *Photo: Henry Georgi*

Photo: *Matt Kuhn*

Summer Story

After the snow liquefies and heads down the watershed, the Cedar Valley turns into a lush green, forested paradise. The jagged peaks of the Lizard Range shed most of their white stuff, leaving a few stubborn pockets on the northern aspects. The unique micro-climate of the Valley again impresses with a combination of hot, southern B.C. weather and ample moisture to sustain a coastal style ecosystem. The old growth forest around Island Lake provides a perfect retreat from the heat of summer and ample opportunity for exploration.

The Valley is home to all the typical Rocky Mountain animals such as moose, mule deer, white-tailed deer, elk, mountain goats, bighorn sheep, black bears, grizzly bears, cougars, lynx, wolverines and wolves. A female moose gives birth on the island almost every spring due to the protection it offers from predators. It's not uncommon to see a dirt streak in the snow of the upper bowls from a grizzly digging itself out of its winter den.

Canoeing on the lake. *Photo: Henry Georgi*

Fernie locals have been enjoying Island Lake since there have been locals. The early 1900s day-use cabin, fishing, berry picking, hunting, hiking and exploring have all lured local residents up to the Cedar Valley over the years.

Unlike winter, you can drive up to the Lodge starting in mid-June. It operates similarly to other mountain lodges found throughout the Rocky Mountains. Accommodation, dining, spectacular hiking and a full spa draw an assortment of visitors. The Bear Lodge patio is one of the most scenic places in the area to have lunch and après hike. The aptly named "I Do Point" provides a popular and stunning place on the Lake to tie the knot.

Island Lake itself may be a bit cold for swimming, but the chilly waters are perfect for the cutthroat trout that inhabit the lake. The Elk River, which runs through Fernie, and a few of its tributaries are considered some of the best fly fishing spots in North America—some say the world. Island Lake is a popular place to stay while exploring the rivers in the area.

Fernie Free Press May 12, 1917
The annual meeting of the Fernie Alpine Club was held on Tuesday evening. The Club has leased Island Lake and the surrounding territory from the Seippel Lumber Co. They are anxious to see the membership increased and hope that all who enjoy going to Island Lake will join, and with this end in view, are providing application blanks, which can be had from any of the officers. Hon. President, F. White; President, Wm. Baldrey; Secretary, C. Muirhead.

A view of Island Lake and the Lizard Range from the Tamarack viewpoint. *Photo: Mike McPhee*

The hiking trails of the Cedar Valley are a summer destination for both locals and visitors. Starting around 2000, a serious effort was made to enhance existing trails and build new ones. A trail crew works hard all summer to keep the trails free and clear and the signage in good shape. Those out for a quick and easy walk will find the Lake Trail to their liking. It takes about an hour to circumnavigate the 2 kilometre trail around the lake. The Rail Trail and Old Growth Trail start lower down in the Valley and make their way to the Lodge from a lower parking lot. The Spineback Trail winds its way up towards Papa Bear Peak, passing through an interesting fossil bed, wild flower meadows and the famous Scot Schmidt tree (from the cover of *P-Tex, Lies and Duct Tape*) at the top of the ridge. Mt. Baldy is a tree-skiing paradise in the winter but in summer holds a great loop with a colourful blanket of mountain wildflowers. Hint: The end of July is the peak of the wildflower bloom. The Tamarack Trail heads up the side ridge of Mount Fernie. Halfway up the ridge is a rocky outcropping called Tamarack Viewpoint; this is one of the best views of the Lizard Range to be had. Heiko's Trail, as it is known (Heiko prefers it to be called The Mountain Lakes Trail), starts 20 kilometres northeast of the Lodge and culminates on the Tamarack Trail, finishing at the Lodge. This is a rigorous, long, day hike and is a signature trail of the Elk Valley.

The annual rhythm continues and summer turns to fall. The tamarack trees turn a deep golden and the Three Bears get a white sprinkle, signalling the coming snow season. As much as summer is loved, catskiing is never far from our minds.

The summit of Big White. *Photo: Mike McPhee*

Fernie Free Press - August 12, 1904
A BEAR STORY

A good bear story is told by one of a crowd of berry pickers who drove out to Lizard Creek on Tuesday to gather blue berries. Mr. A. Milton had found an excellent patch somewhat detached from the others. After a time he heard a rustle but paid no attention to it thinking it was one of his companions. The rustling continued and he called out but got no response. Finally he looked over and saw the head of a brown bear. He went nearer and the bear rose on his hind legs to get a better view of the intruder. He proved to be a monster being, the largest of his kind that Mr. Milton had ever seen. The bear, with a dissatisfied grunt ambled off, but a few minutes later he again made his presence known and this time he evinced no desire to relinquish the fine juicy berries to his visitor and the latter finally drove him off with stones.

Endtro

There is something vitalizing about waking up to snowfall, especially if it started the night before. A quiet energy fills the air with optimism and anticipation. The steady stream of snow falling out the window is hypnotic. These are magical moments that transform you. There are other peaks in other mountain ranges, other pockets of old growth forest, and other lodges in spectacular settings. It seems, though, that the Cedar Valley, little lake with an island and the log lodges all bring together an aesthetically pleasing central point.

Maybe it's because you feel 100 kilometres from the nearest human being, or maybe it's that the peaks of the Three Bears seem so close that you could stretch your arm out to reach them. Whatever that intangible is, it has been felt by most visitors and has left a lasting impression. The character of the place tends to stay with you.

Catskiing may not have been invented at Island Lake Lodge, but a new philosophy of backcountry skiing, snowboarding and general lodge experience was honed and polished there. Island Lake was a key destination during a pivotal moment in the snow industry. It was the blank canvas for a new breed of athlete, filmmaker and powder enthusiast. This trend continues today after earlier groundwork was laid. Skiers and snowboarders learned to coexist and challenge each other there. This is well documented on video and in photos. The unique setting helped inspire some industry leaders, who were changing the focus to big mountains, powder and a new culture of creative freedom on snow. You can't help but feel the spirit of those passed when riding Craig's Line. Seeing the Lizard Range lit up with alpenglow after a day on snow is simply good for the soul. You can't help but feel slightly nostalgic when recognizing one of the many famous photo spots while you're making turns on a ski run. Feeding off this energy is now part of the experience of the place.

Twenty-five years of catskiing may not seem like a long time—especially to those who have been there all along—but it is a worthy milestone within an interesting storyline. Over the years the industry has expanded; backcountry lodges have become much more common. You can go heli- or catskiing just about anywhere now. For those who have experienced Island Lake's magic, and for those who follow snow media and culture—it holds a special place on the mantle. It exists in that ethereal world somewhere between legend, reality and powder-filled dreams. The peaks of the Three Bears still stand tall over the valley, silent sentinels overseeing it all, as they always have and always will.

A night shot of the Tamarack Lodge and the Three Bears basking in an ethereal light. *Photo: Aaron Whitfield*

This book is dedicated to

Craig Kelly - 1966 - 2003
Aiden Oloman - 1976 - 2006

Craig Kelly. *Photo: Mark Gallup*

A very special thanks to:
The Fernie Museum, Mike Pennock, Greg Stump, Scot Schmidt, Ace Mackay-Smith, Beth Gallup, Dan McDonald, Jennie McDonald Krynski, Susan McDonald, Doug Feely, Ian McIntosh, Jeff Patterson, Matt Kuhn, Aaron Whitfield, Henry Georgi, Steve Kuijt, Corrie & Brenda Wright, Dan Savage, John Stifter, Carissa Hart, Dave Treadway, Eric Hjorleifson, Shin Campos, Iain MacMillan, Nick Hamilton, Scott Birke, Dan Egan, Jen McEvenue, Marie-Kristine Landry, Niki LePage, Rick Emmerson, Nick Morris, Steve Kloepzig, Candice Froneman, Sherpas Cinema, Dave Mossop, Eric Crosland, Malcolm Sangster, Patrick Callahan, Jason Ford, Jake Blattner, Heiko and Linda Socher, Reto Keller, all Island Lake staff and guests—past and present.

The authors have tried to the best of their abilities to include as many people and major events as possible. With such a long and complex history some people and or events may have been missed. We thank you in advance for your understanding.

Library and Archives Canada Cataloguing in Publication

McPhee, Mike, 1971

Bears above the valley: a history of catskiing and snowboarding at island lake lodge / Mike McPhee ; Mark Gallup

ISBN 978-0-88982-292-4 I. Title.

We gratefully acknowledge the financial support of the Canada Council for the Arts, the British Columbia Arts Council through the BC Ministry of Tourism, Culture, and the Arts, and the Government of Canada through the Canada Book Fund, for our publishing activities.
Published by
Oolichan Books
P.O. Box 2278
Fernie, British Columbia
Canada V0B 1M0
www.oolichan.com

Printed in Canada